P9-DNA-457

BENJAMIN BRADLEE

That Special Grace

J. B. LIPPINCOTT COMPANY
PHILADELPHIA & NEW YORK

The text of this book originally appeared in Newsweek.

Printed in the United States of America

Library of Congress Catalog Card Number 64-18629

First Edition

Photographic credits in order of appearance: Newsweek; United Press International; Jacques Lowe; George Tames–N.Y. Times; Wide World; David Drew Zingg for Sports Illustrated; Newsweek – Vytas Valaitis; United Press International; Jacques Lowe; Fred Ward – Black Star; European; Jacques Lowe; United Press International; Fred Ward – Black Star; Newsweek – Phil MacMullan.

That Special Grace

History will best judge John F. Kennedy

in calmer days

when time

has made the tragic and the grotesque

at least bearable.

And surely history will judge him well—

for his wisdom and his compassion and his grace.

ENT OF THE

John Kennedy was a wonderfully funny man,

always gay and cheerful,

never mean—

but historians

are prone to stifle laughter in formality.

You could see

a laugh coming in his eyes

before you could hear it from his lips.

His humor was often most appealing
when he directed it against himself.

One summer night in a Georgetown garden,
candidate Kennedy
was preparing for the first
of many critically important appearances
on "Meet the Press."

"You be Kennedy and I'll be Spivak,"
he suggested to his guest with relish,
and the first question
was already spilling forth:

"All right, Horatio Alger,
just what makes you think
you ought to be President?"

Only days ago,
his thoughts turned to the farewell party
for a White House aide
who had been memorialized in print
as "coruscatingly" brilliant.

"Those guys should never forget,"
he said with a smile,
"50,000 votes the other way
and we'd all be coruscatingly stupid."

John Kennedy was a forgiving man,
far more forgiving than his friends.

He forgave many the excesses
of their ignorance—
many men hold high positions today
because of this forgiving.

He forgave quickly and for good,
and soon found new quality in the forgiven.

John Kennedy was a hungry man,
ravenous sometimes
for the nourishment he found
in the life he led
and the people he loved.

This was
both literally and figuratively true.

He could eat
ten bowls of specially prepared fish chowder
without succumbing
to either indigestion or embarrassment,
and though he smoked only rarely,
he could chain-smoke three cigars
when the spirit moved him.

His ability to devour the written word
was legendary,
and he could unwrap presents
faster than a five-year-old.

John Kennedy was a graceful man,

physically graceful

in his movements—

walking, swimming, or swinging a golf club—

and had that special grace of the intellect

that is taste.

He could not bring himself to be "corny"
at a time when "corniness"
is a hallmark of American politics.

On his next-to-last trip,
to the American wilderness,
this compleat and urbane man
was uncomfortable
in the clothes of a conservationist;
and he laughed loudest of all
at the "Paul Bunyan"
or "Johnny Appleseed" nicknames
he quickly collected.

During the 1960 campaign
he used the phrase "Jackie and I" only once,
and that was enough to embarrass him.

He was a student of graceful expression,
and had been since he started
collecting rhetoric in a small black
leather book before the war.

John Kennedy had

a Walter Mitty streak in him,

as wide as his smile.

On the golf course,

when he was winning,

he reminded himself most of Arnold Palmer

in raw power,

or Julius Boros in finesse.

When he was losing,

he was "the old warrior"

at the end of a brilliant career,

asking only that his faithful caddy

point him in the right direction,

and let instinct take over.

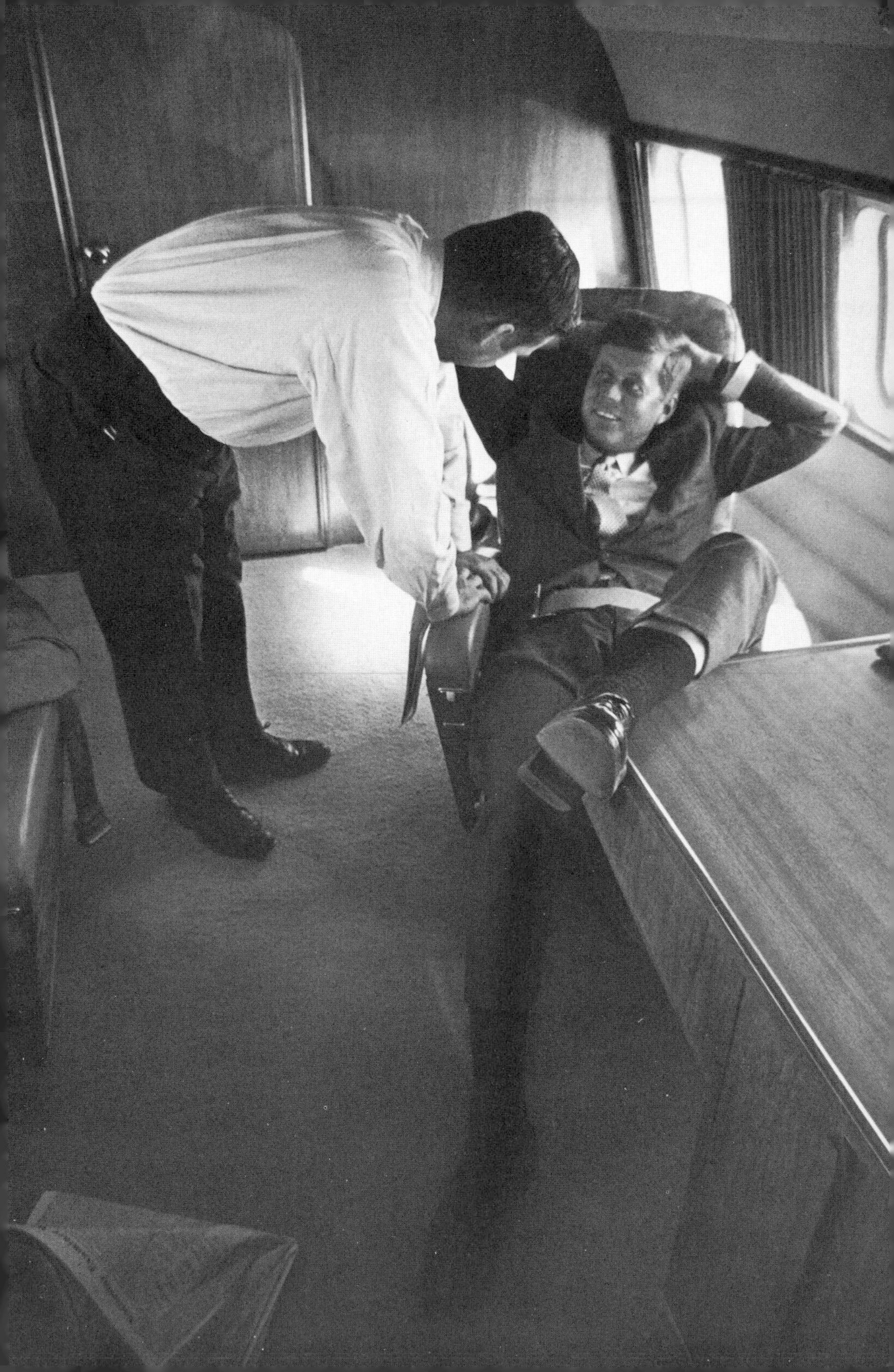

John Kennedy was a restless, exuberant man,
always looking forward
to the next challenge.

For a year now,
it had been "Wait till '64"
more and more often.

And for a long time he had wondered—
at first in fun
but increasingly in seriousness—
what he would do after his second term.

He wondered if he might become
the editor of a newspaper.

He had no real doubt
that he would be re-elected—
hopefully with the mandate
that he missed so much after the 1960 election,
the kind of mandate that would let him do
what he thought the country needed done.

He wanted to run against Goldwater
(though he liked Goldwater personally
more than he liked Rockefeller)
and settle forever
the dangers he saw in standing still.

John Kennedy was a blunt man,
sometimes profane,
when it came to assessing rivals.

But in his judgment,
no man was all bad
who had run for political office,
and by the same token,
every man would be better
if he ran for political office.

He bore no man lasting grudge
or envy,
and his readiness to love
was instinctive.

For John Kennedy was a loving man,
lately come to lasting love.

And historians are too far removed
from love.

John Kennedy reveled in love
for the Irish patrimony
that he had left so far behind.
He laughed with love at the roguery
of his grandfather, Honey Fitz,
and his trip to Ireland
was a pilgrimage to that love.

He loved his brothers and sisters

with a tribal love.

All Kennedys were born gregarious,

but under siege

it could be the Kennedys

against the world.

John Kennedy loved his children
with a light that lit up his world.

He discovered his daughter
when election brought them finally
under the same roof,
and he delighted in her pride
and in her performance.

His heart leapt up when he saw his son,
careening through life
as if there were no tomorrow,
and he lit up the hearts of all
who saw them enjoy each other.

And John Kennedy loved his wife,
who served him so well.

Their life together began as it ended—
in a hospital—
and through sickness and loneliness
there grew the special love
that lights up the soul of the lover
and the loved alike.

John Kennedy is dead,

and for that we are lesser people

in a lesser land.